Almanfaluthi Djaka

Tribal Mandala

Create Your Colorful Expressions

A Coloring Book For Adults

| DEDICATION |

This book is dedicated to my mother, who has always encouraged with me her lovely spirits and compassion to be a survivor. Also to the memory of my father and my brother who were gone too soon. They shared with me a lot of things about this beautiful life. I wish they rest in peace together.

| ACKNOWLEDGMENT |

Special thanks and gratitude to my brothers, family and friends who always encouraged and inspired me to keep my creativity and to complete these artworks. My gratefulness to my ancestors, who called me for a spiritual connection and to come across someone who has been my kindred spirit.

| INTRODUCTION / DIRECTIONS |

Mandala, Tribal, and Unique....these are combined for this coloring book and are connected to the famous sufi poet, Jalaluddin Rumi. I hope it will give new experiences and journeys for coloring, while contemplating his beautiful quotes.
Let this heartfelt meditation help you focus and bring colorful happiness.
Every color has a meaning. After coloring these mandalas, let's be joyful.
Feel free to put colorful creations and expressions on the blank spaces around these mandalas.

In the garden, I see only your face, From trees and blossoms,
I inhale only your fragrance.

~ Jalaluddin Rumi

If the foot of the trees were not tied to earth, they would be pursuing me.
For I have blossomed so much, I am the envy of the gardens.

~ Jalaluddin Rumi

We are the mirror as well as the face in it.
We are tasting the taste this minute of eternity.
We are pain and what cures pain both.
We are the sweet cold water and the jar that pours.

~ Jalaluddin Rumi

Love is a river. Drink from it.

~ Jalaluddin Rumi

A lover's life lies in death. You shall not find a heart without losing the heart.

~ Jalaluddin Rumi

If you were a blade of grass or a tiny flower. I will pitch my tent in your shadow.
Only your presence revives my withered heart.
You are the candle that lights the whole world and I am an empty vessel for your light.

~ Jalaluddin Rumi

Study me as much as you like, you will not know me,
for I differ in a hundred ways from what you see me to be.
Put yourself behind my eyes and see me as I see myself,
for I have chosen to dwell in a place you cannot see.

~ Jalaluddin Rumi

I have come to drag you out of yourself and take you into my heart.
I have come to bring out the beauty you never knew you had,
and lift you like a prayer to the sky.

~ Jalaluddin Rumi

You left ground and sky weeping, mind and soul full of grief. No one can take your place in existence, or in absence. Both mourn, the angels, the prophets, and this sadness I feel has taken from me the taste of language, so that I cannot say the flavor of my being apart.

~ Jalaluddin Rumi

I am weary of personal worrying, in love with the art of madness.

~ Jalaluddin Rumi

Darkness may hide the trees and the flowers from the eyes
but it cannot hide love from the soul.

~ Jalaluddin Rumi

Dance Until You Shatter Yourself.

~ Jalaluddin Rumi

Disappearing from the material world, we reappear in the world of love.
~ Jalaluddin Rumi

Never be without remembrance of Him,
for His remembrance gives strength and wings to the bird of the Spirit.
~ Jalaluddin Rumi

Being a candle is not easy; in order to give light one must burn first.

~ Jalaluddin Rumi

In your light I learn how to love. In your beauty, how to make poems.
You dance inside my chest where no-one sees you, but sometimes I do,
and that sight becomes this art.

~ Jalaluddin Rumi

My heart is so small it's almost invisible. How can You place such big sorrows in it?
"Look," He answered, "your eyes are even smaller, yet they behold the world.

~ Jalaluddin Rumi

Each moment contains a hundred messages from God.
For every cry of "Oh God!" He answers a hundred times "I am Here !"

~ Jalaluddin Rumi

Feel the sweetness in your own heart.
Then you may find the sweetness in every heart.

~ Jalaluddin Rumi

Dance where you can break yourself up to pieces
and totally abandon your worldly passions.

~ Jalaluddin Rumi

The pure heart is a spotless mirror in which images of infinite beauty are reflected.

~ Jalaluddin Rumi

Wherever water flows, life flourishes:
wherever tears fall, Divine mercy is shown.

~ Jalaluddin Rumi

Beauty and Love are as body and soul. Beauty is the mind, Love is the diamond.
They have been together since the beginning of time- Side by side, step by step.

~ Jalaluddin Rumi

When love is not accepted move on;
when love is not appreciated walk away;
hopefully time will teach what real, true love is.

~ Jalaluddin Rumi

The power of love came into me, and I became fierce like a lion,
then tender like the evening star.
~ Jalaluddin Rumi

Goodbyes are only for those who love with their eyes.
Because for those who love with heart and soul there is no such thing as separation.

~ Jalaluddin Rumi

Your heart is the size of an ocean.
Go find yourself in its hidden depths.

~ Jalaluddin Rumi

I will be waiting here, For your silence to break, For your soul to shake
For your love to wake.

~ Jalaluddin Rumi

The soul has no concept of borders, only the concept of love.

~ Jalaluddin Rumi

Wear gratitude like a cloak and it will feed every corner of your life.
~ Jalaluddin Rumi

I want to sing like the birds sing, not worrying about who hears or what they think.
~ Jalaluddin Rumi

Raise your words, not voice. It is rain that grows flowers, not thunder.

~ Jalaluddin Rumi

When you lose all sense of self, the bonds of a thousand chains will vanish.
Lose yourself completely, return to the root of the root of your own soul.

~ Jalaluddin Rumi

What a miracle, You and I, Entwined in the same nest; What a miracle, You and I :
one Love, One Lover, one Fire, In this world and the next, In an ecstasy without end.

~ Jalaluddin Rumi

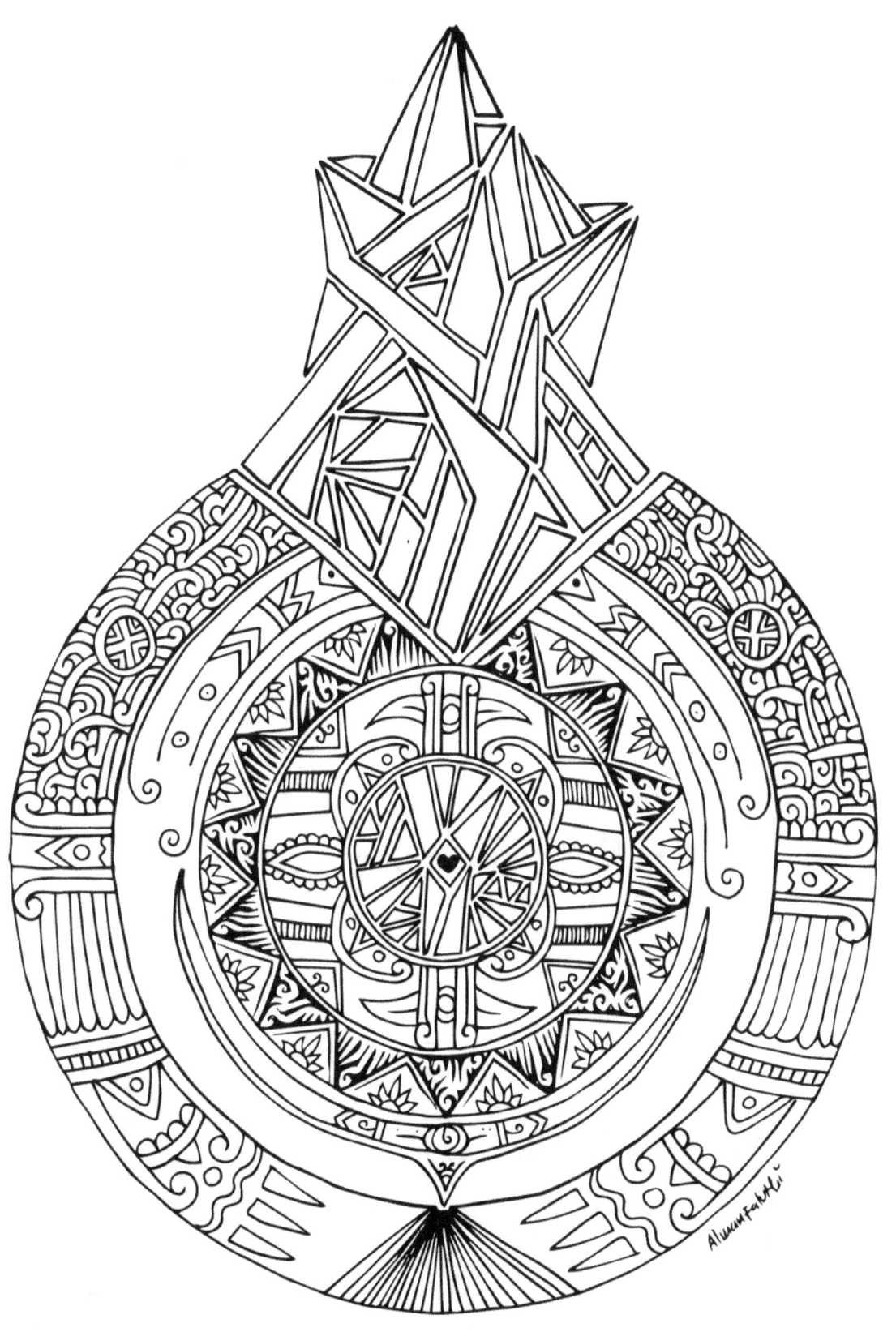

Love is cure, Love is power, Love is the magic of changes.
Love is the mirror of divine beauty.
~ Jalaluddin Rumi

If you find me not within you, you will never find me.
For, I have been with you, from the beginning of me.

~ Jalaluddin Rumi

When love is not accepted move on; when love is not appreciated walk away;
hopefully time will teach what real, true love is.

~ Jalaluddin Rumi

I will whisper secrets in your ear just nod yes and be silent.

~ Jalaluddin Rumi

When setting out on a journey,
do not seek advice from those who have never left. home.

~ Jalaluddin Rumi

God made the illusion look real and the real an illusion.

~ Jalaluddin Rumi

When you lose all sense of self the bonds of a thousand chains will vanish.
Lose yourself completely, return to the root of the root of your own soul.
~ Jalaluddin Rumi

Never lose hope, my heart, miracles dwell in the invisible.

~ Jalaluddin Rumi

Love is the water of life, drink it down with heart and soul.

~ Jalaluddin Rumi

With every breath, I plant the seeds of devotion, I'm a farmer of the heart.

~ Jalaluddin Rumi

Let yourself be silently drawn by the stronger pull of what you really love.
~ Jalaluddin Rumi

Patience is not sitting and waiting, it is foreseeing.
It is looking at the thorn and seeing the rose, looking at the night and seeing the day.
Lovers are patient and know that the moon needs time to become full.

~ Jalaluddin Rumi

Keep walking, though there's no place to get to.
Don't try to see through the distance. That's not for human beings.

~ Jalaluddin Rumi

Love is an emotion, totally silent and inexpressible with words.

~ Jalaluddin Rumi

In your light I learn how to love. In your beauty, how to make poems.
You dance inside my chest where no-one sees you, but sometimes I do,
and that sight becomes this art.

~ Jalaluddin Rumi

Let silence take you to the core of life.

~ Jalaluddin Rumi

Maybe you are searching among the branches, for what only appears in the roots.

~ Jalaluddin Rumi

www.ingramcontent.com/pod-product-compliance
Lightning Source LLC
Chambersburg PA
CBHW081554280526
45788CB00011B/3469